ideals
EASTER

Thou art, O God, the life and light
   Of all this wondrous world we see;
Its glow by day, its smile by night,
   Are but reflections caught from Thee.
Where'er we turn, Thy glories shine,
   And all things fair and bright are Thine.

When day, with farewell beam, delays
   Among the opening clouds of even,
And we can almost think we gaze
   Through opening vistas into heaven,
Those hues that make the sun's decline
   So soft, so radiant, Lord, are Thine.

When night, with wings of starry gloom,
   O'ershadows all the earth and skies,
Like some dark, beauteous bird, whose plume
   Is sparkling with unnumbered eyes,
That sacred gloom, those fires divine,
   So grand, so countless, Lord, are Thine.

When youthful Spring around us breathes,
   Thy spirit warms her fragrant sigh,
And every flower that Summer wreathes
   Is born beneath Thy kindling eye:
Where'er we turn, Thy glories shine,
   And all things fair and bright are Thine.

Thomas Moore

Editorial Director, James Kuse

Managing Editor, Ralph Luedtke

Associate Editor, Colleen Callahan Gonring

Production Editor/Manager, Richard Lawson

Photographic Editor, Gerald Koser

Contributing Editor, Judy A. Turck

ISBN 0-89542-322-7 295

IDEALS—Vol. 36 No. 2, March MCMLXXIX. IDEALS is published eight times a year, January, February, March, May, July, September, November and December—by IDEALS PUBLISHING CORPORATION, 11315 Watertown Plank Road, Milwaukee, Wis. 53226.
Second-class postage paid at Milwaukee, Wisconsin. Copyright © MCMLXXIX by IDEALS PUBLISHING CORPORATION.
All rights reserved. Title IDEALS registered U.S. Patent Office.

ONE YEAR SUBSCRIPTION—eight consecutive issues as published—only $16.00
TWO YEAR SUBSCRIPTION—sixteen consecutive issues as published—only $28.00
SINGLE ISSUES—only $2.95

An Easter Prayer

Lord, now that spring is in the world
And every tulip is a cup
Filled with the wine of thy great love,
Lift thou me up.

Raise thou my heart as flowers arise
To greet the glory of thy day,
With soul as clean as lilies are,
And white as they.

Let me not fear the darkness now,
Since life and light
Break through thy tomb;
Teach me that doubts no more oppress,
No more consume.

Show me that thou art April, Lord,
And thou the flowers and the grass;
Then, when awake the soft spring winds,
I'll hear thee pass!

Charles Hanson Towne

Phtograph opposite
Leland, Wisconsin
Ken Dequaine

The Legend of the Tulips

In medieval times there lived a little old woman who made cheese and peddled it in the nearby village of Devon, England. Although she was poor, she kept her cottage very neat and clean, but she longed for a little beauty and someone to love.

Near the old woman's house lived a wealthy man whose garden bloomed with beautiful, rare tulips of every color. Each day, as the woman passed by the garden on her way to sell her delicious cheese in the village, she dreamed of having one of those blooms in her own yard.

One day she made an especially large cheese, wrapped it carefully and took it up to the large house. She shyly knocked at the door, then boldly asked to see the owner. When the gentleman appeared, the old woman told him of the delicate flavor of her cheese and begged him to try it. After much persuasion, the gentleman sampled the cheese and declared it to be the best he had ever eaten. Pleased, the old woman timidly asked for one precious tulip bulb in payment for the cheese. Afterwards, she hurried home and carefully planted the bulb. Eagerly she awaited spring.

With the warm weather, the old woman daily checked for signs of the green shoots pushing their way up through the soft earth. Sure enough, she was rewarded with a beautiful crimson blossom. The woman stayed home all day just to gaze at her prize beauty.

On an especially cool evening, she was forced to stay inside her house and peer at her tulip. As she strained her eyes through the gathering dusk, to her surprise nestled in the closing petals, she saw a tiny fairy baby fast asleep.

The next day the old woman told a little girl about what she had seen, and soon children came from all around to hear the wonderful story of how the fairies put their babies to bed at night among the tulip blooms.

Each time the old woman made one of her cheeses for the gentleman in the great house, she received a tulip bulb. Soon her yard bloomed with a beauty which surpassed even that of the mansion's garden. And each spring the children came to sit at the old woman's feet and hear the story of how the tulips shelter the fairy babies in the cool, spring evenings.

The beauty of the old woman's garden gained fame far and wide, but even more important to her were the children who filled her yard. For they came not just for the fanciful stories, but also because they loved her.

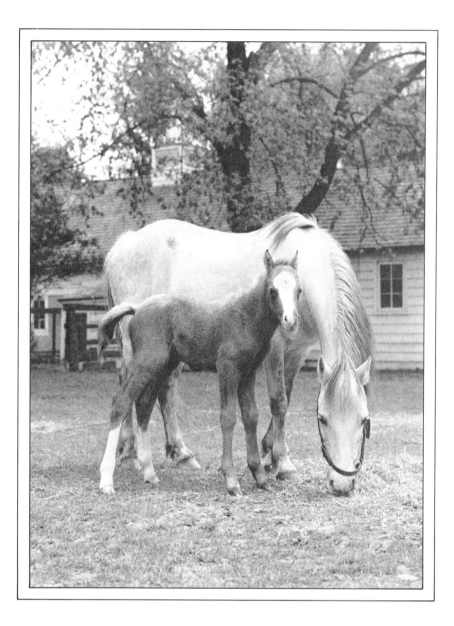

Just at Spring

It seems the world is born anew
When spring first blossoms here,
With tender leaves upon the trees
And skies so bright and clear,
A day in May when buds burst wide,
All nature blossoming.
It happens only once a year
When life is just at spring.

Bright lilacs spread their fragrance rare
Throughout the garden wide;
The orchard, too, is smiling now
Where little creatures hide;
For nature comes alive in spring,
The days are golden bright,
And daylight seems to last and last
Into the still of night.

There's nothing lovelier I know
Than grass all fresh with dew;
Cloud pictures in an April sky
To tell that winter's through.
Each heart and mind then comes alive
To hear the robins sing;
We walk and thrill to nature's charms,
Our world is just at spring.

Garnett Ann Schultz

Photograph opposite
Hollis, New Hampshire
Fred Sieb

The Feast of St. Patrick

The life of St. Patrick is surrounded by legend; and many scholars believe he is a composite of several early missionaries to Ireland. What is known is that around the fifth century, a man now called St. Patrick was traveling around Ireland, diligently spreading the word of Christianity.

St. Patrick understood the superstitious nature of a people dominated by barbarian chieftains, and Druid priests. He attracted their attention and imagination by beating a drum as he traveled and preached. Legend says that with the help of this drum, St. Patrick drove all the snakes out of Ireland. According to another legend, this celebrated priest courageously defied a barbarian chief's decree against signal fires and lit a great fire, proclaiming the light of Christianity would blaze forever.

St. Patrick's reputation still blazes and through his preaching he baptized countless persons, and established churches and schools. Even today, the feast of St. Patrick is commemorated in Ireland by attending mass in his honor; and March 17 is a national holiday celebrated with parades, dances and merrymaking.

As the Irish emigrated, they took the traditions of St. Patrick to other countries of the world. Being a warmhearted people, they welcomed all to join in the festivities and the "wearin'-of-the-green" on March 17.

St. Patrick's Day is not just a great day for the Irish, but a day observed with much enthusiasm by everyone. This is the day for Irish music and Irish jigs. Shamrocks, shillelaghs, and shenanigans abound, and the luck of the Irish is shared by all!

When Irish Eyes Are Smiling

Chauncey Olcott
George Graff, Jr.

There's a tear in your eye,
And I'm wondering why,
For it never should be there at all.
With such pow'r in your smile,
Sure a stone you'd beguile,
So there's never a teardrop should fall.
When your sweet lilting laughter's
Like some fairy song,
And your eyes twinkle bright as can be;
You should laugh all the while
And all other times smile
And now smile a smile for me.

When Irish eyes are smiling,
Sure it's like a morn in spring.
In the lilt of Irish laughter,
You can hear the angels sing.
When Irish hearts are happy
All the world seems bright and gay,
And when Irish eyes are smiling,
Sure they steal your heart away.

For your smile is a part
Of the love in your heart,
And it makes even sunshine more bright.
Like the linnets' sweet song,
Crooning all the day long,
Comes your laughter so tender and light.
For the springtime of life
Is the sweetest of all,
There is ne'er a real care or regret;
And while springtime is ours
Throughout all of youth's hours,
Let us smile each chance we get.

An Apple Orchard
in the Spring

Have you seen an apple orchard in the spring?
    In the spring?
An English apple orchard in the spring?
   When the spreading trees are hoary
   With their wealth of promised glory,
   And the mavis sings its story,
    In the spring.

Have you plucked the apple blossoms in the spring?
    In the spring?
And caught their subtle odors in the spring?
   Pink buds pouting at the light,
   Crumpled petals baby-white,
   Just to touch them a delight,
    In the spring.

Have you walked beneath the blossoms in the spring?
   In the spring?
Beneath the apple blossoms in the spring?
  When the pink cascades are falling,
  And the silver brooklets brawling,
  And the cuckoo bird soft calling,
   In the spring.

If you have not, then you know not, in the spring,
    In the spring,
Half the color, beauty, wonder of the spring,
   No sweet sight can I remember
   Half so precious, half so tender,
   As the apple blossoms render
    In the spring.

William Martin

Photograph opposite
Grant Heilman

Robin's Come

From the elm tree's topmost bough,
  Hark! the robin's early song!
Telling one and all that now
  Merry springtime hastes along;
Welcome tidings dost thou bring,
  Little harbinger of spring;
    Robin's come!

  Of the winter we are weary,
    Weary of the frost and snow,
  Longing for the sunshine cheery,
    And the brooklet's gurgling flow;
  Gladly, then, we hear thee sing
    The reveille of the spring,
      Robin's come!

Ring it out o'er hill and plain,
  Through the garden's lonely bowers,
Till the green leaves dance again,
  Till the air is sweet with flowers!
Wake the cowslips by the rill,
  Wake the yellow daffodil!
    Robin's come!

Then, as thou wert wont of yore,
  Build thy nest and rear thy young
Close beside our cottage door,
  In the woodbine leaves among;
Hurt or harm thou need'st not fear,
  Nothing rude shall venture near.
    Robin's come!

William W. Caldwell

An Easter Carol

Spring bursts today,
For Christ is risen and all the earth's at play

Flash forth, thou sun.
The rain is over and gone, its work is done.

Winter is past,
Sweet spring is come at last, is come at last.

Bud, fig, and vine,
Bud, olive, fat with fruit, and oil, and wine.

Break forth this morn
In roses, thou but yesterday a thorn.

Uplift thy head,
O pure white lily, through the winter dead.

Beside your dams
Leap and rejoice, you merrymaking lambs.

All herds and flocks
Rejoice, all beasts of thickets and of rock.

Sing, creatures, sing,
Angels, and men, and birds, and everything.

Christina G. Rossetti

Mr. Easter Rabbit

A long time ago, in a far-off country, there was a famine; and this is how it came about: In the early spring, when the first grass peeped out, the sun shone so hot that the grass was dried up. No rains fell through the long summer months, so that the seed and grain that were planted could not grow, and everywhere the fields and meadows—usually so green and rich—were a dull gray-brown.

Here and there a green tree waved its dusty branches in the hot wind. When fall came, instead of the well-filled granaries and barns, there was great emptiness; and instead of happy fathers and mothers, there were grave, troubled ones.

But the children were just as happy as ever. They were glad, even, that it had not rained, for they could play out-of-doors all day long; and the dust-piles had never been so large and fine.

The people had to be very saving of the things that had been left from the year before. All the following winter, by being very careful, they managed to provide simple food for their families. When Christmas came there were not many presents, but the children did not miss them as we would, because in that land they did not give many presents at Christmastime.

Their holiday was Easter Sunday. On that day they had a great celebration, and there were always goodies and presents for the little boys and girls. As the time came nearer, the parents wondered what they should do for the children's holiday. Every new day it was harder than the day before to get just plain, coarse bread to eat; and where would they find all the sweetmeats and pretty things that the children had always had at Eastertime?

One evening some of the mothers met, after the children were in bed, to talk about what they should do. One mother said: "We can have eggs. All the chickens are laying; but the children are tired of eggs for they have them every day."

So they decided that eggs would never do for an Easter treat; and they went home sorrowfully, thinking that Easter must come and go like any other day. And one mother was more sorry than any of the others. Her dear little boy and girl had been planning and talking about the beautiful time they were to have on the great holiday.

After the mother had gone to bed, she wondered and thought if there were any way by which she could give her little ones their happy time. All at once she cried right out in the dark: "I know! I have thought of something to make the children happy!"

She could hardly wait until morning, and the first thing she did was to run into the next house and tell her neighbor of the bright plan she had thought of. And the neighbor told someone else, and so the secret flew until, before night, all the mothers had heard it, but not a single child.

There was still a week before Easter, so there was a good deal of whispering; and the fathers and mothers smiled every time they thought of the secret. When Easter Sunday came, everyone went, first of all, to the great stone church—mothers and fathers and children. When church was over, instead of going home, the older people suggested walking to the great woods just back of the church.

"Perhaps we may find some flowers," they said.

So on they went, and soon the merry children were scattered through the woods, among the trees.

Then a shout went up—now here, now there—from all sides.

"Father, Mother, look here!"

"See what I have found—some beautiful eggs!"

"Here's a red one!"

"I've found a yellow one!"

"Here's a whole nestful—all different colors!"

And the children came running, bringing beautiful colored eggs which they had found in the soft moss under the trees. What kind of eggs could they be? They were too large for bird's eggs; they were large, like hens' eggs; but who ever saw a hen's egg so wonderfully colored?

Just then, from behind a large tree where the children had found a nest full of eggs, there jumped a rabbit, and with long leaps he disappeared in the deep woods, where he was hidden from view by the trees and the bushes.

"It must be that the rabbit laid the pretty eggs," said one little girl.

"I am sure it was the rabbit," said her mother.

"Hurrah for the rabbit! Hurrah for the Easter rabbit! Hurrah for Mr. Easter Rabbit!" the children cried; and the fathers and mothers were glad with the children.

So this is the story of the first Easter eggs, for, ever since then, in that faraway land and in other countries, too, has Mr. Easter Rabbit brought the children at Eastertime some beautiful colored eggs.

Carolyn Sherwin Bailey

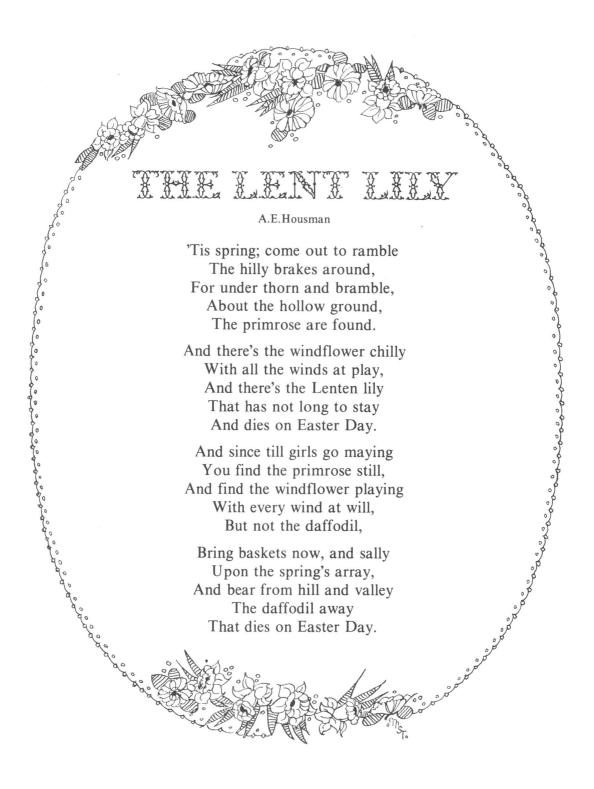

THE LENT LILY

A.E. Housman

’Tis spring; come out to ramble
The hilly brakes around,
For under thorn and bramble,
About the hollow ground,
The primrose are found.

And there’s the windflower chilly
With all the winds at play,
And there’s the Lenten lily
That has not long to stay
And dies on Easter Day.

And since till girls go maying
You find the primrose still,
And find the windflower playing
With every wind at will,
But not the daffodil,

Bring baskets now, and sally
Upon the spring’s array,
And bear from hill and valley
The daffodil away
That dies on Easter Day.

Photograph opposite
Robert Cushman Hayes

The Day before April

The day before April
  Alone, alone,
I walked in the woods
  And sat on a stone.

I sat on a broad stone
  And sang to the birds.
The tune was God's making
  But I made the words.

Mary Carolyn Davies

Reprinted by permission of Laura Benét.

Each Year

Can spring be far away when robins call;
  When snowmen gradually withdraw from sight;
When wild geese soar high in northward flight;
  When snows melt beneath the gentle rainfall?
Today I saw, behind the garden wall,
  Pale green shoots coming into light,
As if awakened only just last night.
  I know the earth keeps life in all.
Somehow, I know when spring is close at hand;
  For I feel within my heart a glow
Of warmth that only special time can bring.
  I see changing colors on the land
Where violets and yellow jasmine grow.
  Each year brings forth a bright, new birth of spring.

May Smith White

The Lore of the Easter Bunny

For children in Germany, Easter Eve is an exciting time; for it is on this night that the *Osterhase*, or Easter Bunny, will visit the homes of those children who have been very good all year. Boys and girls of all ages go to bed early, believing that the *Osterhase* will bring beautifully colored eggs.

Of course, it is really the mother who secretly boils, dyes and decorates the eggs; then, with the father, hides them throughout the house.

On Easter morning when the children awaken, they are anxious to discover if the white hare paid them a visit and if they can find his hidden treasures. Just as they begin to suspect the *Osterhase* has passed them by, they spot one egg, then another, and soon another, until finally all the eggs are found. The children are delighted because they know that they have been good indeed.

Here in America, the *Osterhase* is known as the Easter Bunny. By whatever name, he is still welcomed for the beautiful eggs he brings to good little children on Easter Sunday.

Photograph opposite
Grant Heilman

Georgia B. Adams

Georgia B. Adams has been writing poetry for over thirty years. The Pennsylvania-born writer acquired an appreciation for poetry at an early age, and began writing when she was twelve years old. Edgar A. Guest has been a major source of inspiration for Miss Adams' work. Never intending to write poetry for profit, Miss Adams has, nevertheless, written and published over 2,700 poems, provided the lyrics for 150 hymns, and written the words for a Christmas cantata which was published and performed in 1966. *The Silver Flute*, published in 1968, is an anthology of her poems. International recognition came when Miss Adams was officially listed in the International Who's-Who in Poetry for 1974-75. Besides her prolific writing, Miss Adams has been employed for the past twenty-six years as a communications specialist. For many years, Miss Adams has contributed several hundred of her poems to Ideals publications. The following are a sampling of her fine literary work.

Happiness Is Spring

Happiness is a day in spring
  When pussy willows pop,
When rabbits in my yard are tame,
  And frisk and jump and hop.

Happiness is when crocuses
  Break through the crust of sod,
When stooping down to see them close
  I catch a glimpse of God.

Happiness is when robins sing
  Concertos in the trees,
When scents of chubby hyacinths
  Waft on the gentle breeze.

Happiness is when spring is here
  And all around you see
The gifts of nature manifest
  And immortality.

It's Spring!

It's spring and the robins are singing
  Their roundelays, one, two, three;
My heart is as happy as ever
  Just skipping with mirth and glee!

I've discovered the pussy willows
  All plushy and "kittenish";
The day is just full of surprises
  From its very start to its finish.

The crocuses have been poking
  Their heads of purple and gold
Above the sod, and I dare say,
  An awesome sight to behold.

The geese have been flying over;
  My heart tells me it is true
That spring is coming, it's coming!
  I love this season, don't you?

Springtime Melody

Springtime is like a melody,
  Its gayest notes impart
A brand new lease on life again,
  Much joy to every heart.

It sings with every blooming flower,
  It hums with every breeze,
And robins sing their arias
  High up in greening trees.

It vocalizes with a sky
  That's blue and cloudless, too;
It serenades when raindrops fall
  And in the drops of dew.

Springtime is like a melody,
  Its gay song thrills each heart.
And I'm right there to take it in
  When springtime gets its start.

The Call of the Earth

I walk through the woods in springtime
  To hear the call of the earth,
To blossom, to bud, to flower
  In a glad, wholesome rebirth.

The chestnuts, the elms, the maples
  Are now a feathery green;
The bloodroot violet grows there,
  Still lovelier than I've seen.

I see the sky through the treetops
  All scattered with cloud puffs there;
I feel the warmth of the sun's rays
  Though there's still a chill to the air.

That damsel so sweet called April
  Is filling the air with mirth!
I walk through the woods this fine day
  To hear the call of the earth.

Song of Spring

I heard the song of spring today;
  It whispered through the trees,
It rose up to the skies above,
  'Twas carried by the breeze.

I wondered where the sound came from;
  And on the fence I saw
A plump red robin sing
  His song without a flaw!

His world was bright and so was mine,
  He seemed to give to me
A new beginning and a song
  That bubbled happily.

I heard the song of spring today!
  Look up; you, too, shall see
The robin, and you, too, shall hear
  His song of ecstasy!

Succession

Hal Borland

There is a succession in the days, now, that quickens the human heart. Whether they are gusty days or days of calm, chill days or days of deepening warmth, they have the air of change. No two days are alike. Sometimes it seems as though the season were trying a variety of moods, playacting in a dozen different parts, eager to be spring and reluctant to be no longer winter. But the very indecision is itself the mark of change.

The hardy plants of spring reflect the trend. Daffodils are well up and hyacinths have broken ground. Crocuses have spread the color to the temperamental winds. Beneath their mulch, the peonies are showing pips of crimson. Flower buds are so fat on the forsythia that when a shoot is brought indoors its golden bells open almost overnight. Iris sends up its green bayonets. And mountain pink is full of fat buds awaiting only a few successive days of April sun. There is the amber glow, luminous and almost translucent, in the willow withes.

You walk through the garden, still largely bare and waiting, and you see these things. And you look down a long hillside and you feel them, feel the pressure of succession, the slow but certain urge of change. Growth is there in the earth, at the grass roots, at the twig ends. The green world is waiting, already in the making where the mysterious chemistry of sap and chlorophyll has its origins. And the heart responds, already sensing the seedling, the new shoot, the summer's dappled shade. April whispers from the hilltop, even as March goes whistling down the valley.

Sing Hosanna!

They brought Him a colt to ride on;
Spread their garments at His feet.
"Blessed be the kingdom of David!"
Came the shout on the palm-covered street.

"Hosanna! to the son of David,
He who comes in the name of the Lord!
Bless His name!" they shouted before Him.
"Hosanna!" cried the gathering crowd.

"Rebuke them! Rebuke your disciples!"
Yelled the Pharisees, mingling about.
He answered, "If these were silent,
Then the very stones would cry out."

Then spoke the Pharisees, wisely,
"Nothing at all can we do.
The whole world follows after Him!
They call Him the King of the Jews!"

Sing hosanna in the highest!
Spread branches of palms in the way!
The King is riding in glory.
Come, let us praise Him today!

Alice Leedy Mason

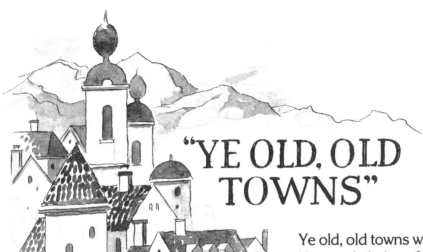

"YE OLD, OLD TOWNS"

Ye old, old towns with your turrets and steeples,
Your red-tiled roofs, resting sepal on sepal,
Your cobblestone streets and balcony flowers,
Statues and parks and medieval towers;
Yours is a culture preserving the best.
Centuries old, your worth will attest.
Yours are a people who dance and who sing,
Who out of their winters always find spring.

Old as your histories, old as your wars,
Old as your forests, your valleys, your stars,
Yet when spring comes—as springs wont to do—
Old worlds of splendor will blossom anew.
Ring then ye bells; God reigns in these mountains,
While fables and myths surround castle and fountain.
Green then ye lindens and sing then ye linnets,
While ancient old clocks tick minute by minute.

Nest, too, ye storks on old chimney tops;
Terraces green to vineyards and hops.
Grow, too, ye gardens, ye green fields of grain;
Somewhere a cuckoo is calling again.
Somewhere a swallow is building of yore;
Violets and woodrush are fragrant once more.
Somewhere spring rain is falling in sheets;
Wooden shoes clatter again in your streets.
Beckon once more, ye turrets, ye steeples;
Yours is the home of my mother's good people.

Minnie Klemme

Phtograph opposite
Church at the base of Kaiser Mountain, Tirol, Austria
Josef Muench

Spring

Now fades the last long streak of snow,
    Now bourgeons every maze of quick
About the flowering squares, and thick
    By ashen roots the violets blow.

    Now rings the woodland loud and long,
        The distance takes a lovelier hue,
    And drowned in yonder living blue
        The lark becomes a sightless song.

    Now dance the lights on lawn and lea,
        The flocks are whiter down the vale,
    And milkier every milky sail
        On winding stream or distant sea;

Where now the sea-mew pipes, or dives
    In yonder greening gleam, and fly
The happy birds, that change their sky
    To build and brood, that live their lives

    From land to land; and in my breast
        Spring wakens too; and my regret
    Becomes an April violet,
        And buds and blossoms like the rest.

Alfred, Lord Tennyson

Photograph opposite
Jack-in-the-pulpit
Alpha Photo Associates

The Easter Story

Entry Into Jerusalem

And when they drew nigh unto Jerusalem, and were come to Bethphage, unto the mount of Olives, then sent Jesus two disciples, saying unto them, Go into the village over against you, and straightway ye shall find an ass tied, and a colt with her: loose them, and bring them unto me. And if any man say ought unto you, ye shall say, The Lord hath need of them; and straightway he will send them.

All this was done, that it might be fulfilled which was spoken by the prophet, saying, Tell ye the daughter of Sion, Behold, thy King cometh unto thee, meek, and sitting upon an ass, and a colt the foal of an ass. And the disciples went, and did as Jesus commanded them, And brought the ass, and the colt, and put on them their clothes, and they set him thereon.

And a very great multitude spread their garments in the way; others cut down branches from the trees, and strawed them in the way. And the multitudes that went before, and that followed, cried, saying Hosanna to the Son of David: Blessed is he that cometh in the name of the Lord; Hosanna in the highest. And when he was come into Jerusalem, all the city was moved, saying, Who is this? And the multitude said, This is Jesus the prophet of Nazareth of Galilee.

Matthew 21:1-11

Painting opposite
ENTRANCE INTO JERUSALEM
by Dalsgaard
Photo, Three Lions, Inc.

The Last Supper

And the first day of unleavened bread, when they killed the Passover, his disciples said unto him, Where wilt thou that we go and prepare that thou mayest eat the Passover? And he sendeth forth two of his disciples, and saith unto them, Go ye into the city, and there shall meet you a man bearing a pitcher of water: follow him. And wheresoever he shall go in, say ye to the goodman of the house, The Master saith, Where is the guest-chamber, where I shall eat the Passover with my disciples? And he will shew you a large upper room furnished and prepared: there make ready for us. And his disciples went forth, and came into the city, and found as he had said unto them: and they made ready the Passover.

And in the evening he cometh with the twelve. And as they sat and did eat, Jesus said, Verily I say unto you, One of you which eateth with me shall betray me. And they began to be sorrowful, and to say unto him one by one, Is it I? and another said, Is it I? And he answered and said unto them, It is one of the twelve, that dippeth with me in the dish. The Son of man indeed goeth, as it is written of him: but woe to that man by whom the Son of man is betrayed! good were it for that man if he had never been born. And as they did eat, Jesus took bread, and blessed, and brake it, and gave to them, and said, Take, eat: this is my body. And he took the cup, and when he had given thanks, he gave it to them: and they all drank of it. And he said unto them, This is my blood of the new testament, which is shed for many. Verily I say unto you, I will drink no more of the fruit of the vine, until that day that I drink it new in the kingdom of God.

Mark 14:12-25

Agony at Gethsemane

And they came to a place which was named Geth-sem-a-ne: and he saith to his disciples, Sit ye here, while I shall pray. And he taketh with him Peter and James and John, and began to be sore amazed, and to be very heavy; And saith unto them, My soul is exceeding sorrowful unto death: tarry ye here, and watch. And he went forward a little, and fell on the ground, and prayed that, if it were possible, the hour might pass from him. And he said, Abba, Father, all things are possible unto thee; take away this cup from me: nevertheless not what I will, but what thou wilt.

And he cometh, and findeth them sleeping, and saith unto Peter, Simon, sleepest thou? couldest not thou watch one hour? Watch ye and pray, lest ye enter into temptation. The spirit truly is ready, but the flesh is weak. And again he went away, and prayed, and spake the same words. And when he returned, he found them asleep again, (for their eyes were heavy,) neither wist they what to answer him.

And he cometh the third time, and saith unto them, Sleep on now, and take your rest: it is enough, the hour is come; behold, the Son of man is betrayed into the hands of sinners. Rise up, let us go; lo, he that betrayeth me is at hand.

Mark 14:32-42

Painting opposite
CHRIST PRAYING IN GETHSEMANE
by Schielssner
Photo, Three Lions, Inc.

The Way of the Cross

Then released he Barabbas unto them: and when he had scourged Jesus, he delivered him to be crucified. Then the soldiers of the governor took Jesus into the common hall, and gathered unto him the whole band of soldiers. And they stripped him, and put on him a scarlet robe. And when they had platted a crown of thorns, they put it upon his head, and a reed in his right hand: and they bowed the knee before him, and mocked him, saying, Hail, King of the Jews! And they spit upon him, and took the reed, and smote him on the head.

And after that they had mocked him, they took the robe off from him, and put his own raiment on him, and led him away to crucify him. And as they came out, they found a man of Cyrene, Simon by name: him they compelled to bear his cross.

Matthew 27:26-32

Painting opposite
JESUS UNDER THE BURDEN OF HIS CROSS
by S. Del Piambo
Photo, Three Lions, Inc.

The Crucifixion

And when they were come to the place, which is called Calvary, there they crucified him, and the malefactors, one on the right hand, and the other on the left. Then said Jesus, Father, forgive them; for they know not what they do. And they parted his raiment, and cast lots. And the people stood beholding. And the rulers also with them deriding him, saying, He saved others; let him save himself, if he be Christ, the chosen of God. And the soldiers also mocked him, coming to him, and offering him vinegar. And saying, If thou be the king of the Jews, save thyself. And a superscription also was written over him in letters of Greek, and Latin, and Hebrew, *This Is the King of the Jews.* And one of the malefactors which were hanged railed on him, saying, If thou be Christ, save thyself and us. But the other answering rebuked him, saying, Dost not thou fear God, seeing thou art in the same condemnation? And we indeed justly; for we receive the due reward of our deeds: but this man hath done nothing amiss. And he said unto Jesus, Lord, remember me when thou comest into thy kingdom. And Jesus said unto him, Verily I say unto thee, Today shalt thou be with me in paradise.

And it was about the sixth hour, and there was a darkness over all the earth until the ninth hour. And the sun was darkened, and the veil of the temple was rent in the midst. And when Jesus had cried with a loud voice, he said, Father, into thy hands I commend my spirit: and having said thus, he gave up the ghost.

Luke 23:33-46

The Resurrection

In the end of the Sabbath, as it began to dawn toward the first day of the week, came Mary Magdalene and the other Mary to see the sepulchre. And, behold, there was a great earthquake: for the angel of the Lord descended from heaven, and came and rolled back the stone from the door, and sat upon it. His countenance was like lightning, and his raiment white as snow: And for fear of him the keepers did shake, and became as dead men.

And the angel answered and said unto the women, Fear not ye: for I know that ye seek Jesus, which was crucified. He is not here: for he is risen, as he said, Come, see the place where the Lord lay. And go quickly, and tell his disciples that he is risen from the dead; and, behold, he goeth before you into Galilee; there shall ye see him: lo, I have told you. And they departed quickly from the sepulchre with fear and great joy; and did run to bring his disciples word.

Matthew 28:1-8

Painting opposite
THE RESURRECTION
by Anton Dorph
Photo, Three Lions, Inc.

Empty Tomb, Full Heart

How can I describe the emotions flooding my soul as I wait my turn to enter the Garden Tomb, the place where Jesus Christ defeated death?

Although I am a writer, at this moment I have difficulty finding even one phrase to describe this moment. Perhaps the words "a quiet excitement" convey some of my feelings. I glance over at my daughter and the other forty-three members of our tour group from the United States, and their faces mirror my own keen anticipation; but each person is quiet and reflective. Someone breaks the silence with a soft melodic strain—a song by Bill Gaither. Somehow this hymn takes on a fresh meaning here in the shade of the Garden Tomb north of Damascus Gate, and soon many voices join in the singing:

Because He lives, I can face tomorrow;
Because He lives, all fear is gone;
Because I know, yes I know He holds the future,
And life is worth the living
Just because He lives.

The singing ends but the words remain in my heart. I am gripped by the knowledge that this is the place where the angels declared, "He is not here but is risen!"

Archaeological discoveries and biblical descriptions of the tomb verify my conviction that this is, indeed, the tomb of Christ. As recent as 1970, the great British archaeologist Dame Kathleen Kenyon stated, "It is a typical tomb of about the first centry A.D." Other archaeologists concluded the tomb belonged to a wealthy Jew of the Herodian period; and Matthew 27:57 states the tomb belonged to Joseph of Arimathea, a rich and honorable member of the Sanhedrin, the Supreme Council of the Jews. Matthew further states that Christ's burial place was hewn in a rock; and upon observation, it is clear that this is not just an old cave adapted as a burial place; but a tomb dug out of the rock.

The biblical record of John places the tomb in a garden near the place of the crucifixion. Once again, this tomb fits the biblical description, as Golgotha is a very short distance from the Garden Tomb. Luke described it as spacious enough for a number of persons to stand inside and Matthew further pictures it as being sealed with "a great stone." In all detail the Garden Tomb fulfills the scriptural record.

Inside the tomb, the visitors note the ledges on each side of the tomb entrance, perhaps indicating a vaulted roof of an early church erected in front. To the left of the door is an anchor, an early Christian symbol, etched in the rock face.

As fascinating as these facts are, it is my spirit, not my mind, that registers the wonder of the empty tomb. Gone is the feeling of dissolution I sensed when I visited the other sites of biblical events. Here I sense an overpowering truth: Jesus did die; he was buried; but he rose the third day according to the Scriptures.

At last our turn has come to go in. The other group is leaving and I step closer to the tomb. I stand at the entrance to this Garden Tomb, and although I am only five feet four inches tall, I must bow low to enter. Directly in front of me is the "weeping chamber." To my right is the low opening leading to the graves. As I walk over the threshold, I see the burial place with a pillow cut in the rock, and I say to myself, "This is where your Savior tasted death for every man. This is where he triumphed over death and the grave!" The words of Robert Lowry took on special meaning:

Up from the grave he arose!
With a mighty triumph o'er His foes!
He arose a victor from the dark domain,
And He lives forever with His saints to reign!
He arose! He arose!
Hallelujah! Christ arose!

The Empty Tomb   Rev. John Rohrer

It is now time to return, and as I step from the tomb into the cool, crisp air of this February morning, I know I will never again be the same. For me, the resurrection has been verified by physical evidence and the Lord's promise is clear. He said, "Because I live, you too shall live!" If death could not hold him, it will not hold me. When my spirit is released from this body, I will live forever with God.

Well over a year has passed since my visit to the Garden Tomb, but I still feel "a quiet excitement" as I remember Christ's triumph over death, and I try to share this hope with others. The eternal hope as expressed in Romans 1:4, "[Jesus Christ] declared to be the Son of God with power, according to the spirit of holiness, by the resurrection from the dead."

As we look forward to Easter 1979, with its reminders of everlasting life, I would like to share some lines I wrote shortly after my return from the Holy Land. May they help to make this Easter even more meaningful to you.

I have seen the empty tomb;
I've stood amazed and hushed
In the holy presence of Him
Who conquers death and hell and gloom.
He is not here! O symphony of victory!
He is not here! Forevermore He lives!
My heart is thrilled with the peace,
The joy, the glory that only Jesus gives.

Nathanael Olson

Where Wild
Flowers Grow

I love the spots where wild flowers grow;
The kinds we never have to sow,
A gift of God beneath his sky
To thrill the hearts of passersby.

I love the violets, small and dear
That mark the springtime of our year,
Within the grass, so oft not seen,
And yet so dainty, like a dream.

The daisies hold a special place,
A heart of gold that's trimmed with lace,
That small girls pick along their way
To make a dainty bright bouquet.

The dandelions everywhere
As bright as gold on springtime air;
The world loves roses, this I know,
But my heart loves where wild flowers grow.

Garnett Ann Schultz

Photograph opposite
Hepatica, Sharplobe
Alpha Photo Associates

Desert Magic

Through heat-swept sands I walked one day
And knew a stillness touched with gray,
Shadows clinging to the sage
Between soft sand dunes, rooted well in age.

No brightness touched my foot or hand
To strike a melody in that land
Where life was silent and unheard.

Suddenly, as though by some molten word,
The wastelands blossomed—flung gay
Laughter down the sands once robed in gray,
And once again, spring passed this way.

James Neill Northe

Photograph opposite
Apache Trail, Arizona
David Muench

The lore of the Easter lily is a combination of myth and symbol in connection with Christ's Resurrection. As one of the spring flowers, it represents the renewal of life and the rebirth of the spirit. This symbolic association has its origin in the flowers which existed in the Holy Land during Christ's passion and death.

According to legend, on the night before Christ's death, the lily lost its self-esteem when it failed to join the other flowers and bow its head in sorrow as Christ passed through the garden of Gethsemane. For the lily considered itself the most beautiful and most fragrant flower in the garden. After seeing Christ's humility, the lily belatedly bent its head in shame, and has remained in this humble attitude ever since.

Our Easter lily is not native to Palestine, but was imported from the island of Bermuda in the 1880s. Called the Croft's Lily, it is grown mainly in the Pacific Northwest and California. Every year, in hothouses across the country, millions of these bulbs are forced to bloom in time for the Easter season.

The
Easter Lily

The Flowers of Easter

Nancy Byrd Turner

They have come back to field and hill,
    To garden and to wood,
The crocus and the daffodil,
    The violet in her hood,
The mignonette, the pansy blue,
    The lily straight and tall;
So like the flowers, dewy, still,
    In that old garden on a hill,
The first Easter of all!

        I think the light, that morning, fell
            In the same lovely way
        On petal, leaf, and lifting bell,
            As the light falls today;
        That violets looked gently up,
            Hearing the dawn-wind's call,
        And dew was in a crocus cup
            And fragrance in a lily cup,
        In that old garden long ago,
            The first Easter of all.

All Things
Bright and Beautiful

All things bright and beautiful,
    All creatures great and small,
All things wise and wonderful,
    The Lord God made them all.

Each little flower that opens,
    Each little bird that sings,
He made their glowing colours,
    He made their tiny wings.

The rich man in his castle,
    The poor man at his gate,
God made them, high or lowly,
    And order'd their estate.

The purple-headed mountain,
    The river running by,
The sunset and the morning,
    That brightens up the sky;

The cold wind in the winter,
    The pleasant summer sun,
The ripe fruits in the garden,
    He made them every one.

The tall trees in the greenwood,
    The meadows where we play,
The rushes by the water
    We gather every day;

He gave us eyes to see them,
    And lips that we might tell,
How great is God Almighty,
    Who has made all things well.

Cecil Frances Alexander

Photograph opposite
Fred Sieb

# Holidays

Catherine Otten

Since New Year's Day was always celebrated as a part of the Christmas season, Easter was the first holiday to emerge out of the bitter cold days of winter.

In our neighborhood, our little store was the official announcer of the coming of all holidays. With the beginning of Lent, fresh smoked fish, kegs of herring, more kinds of cheese than usual, and Mama's special herring roll-mops were prominently displayed to help make the many obligated meatless meals easier to bear.

The candy window, always the headliner of displays, was full of pink and white and chocolate marshmallow rabbits and eggs. Soft yellow, sugary chicks lay in neat rows between the solid milk chocolate rabbits, elegant in their shiny gold and silver foil wrappers. Tall glass jars of jelly beans decorated the back shelves of the candy corner. Tiny tin frying pans containing creamy candy sunny-side-up fried eggs, and other Easter novelties at a penny each were lined up on the top shelves of the glass candy case. The Easter rabbit was an experienced expert at displaying his sweet wares.

These were days of fast and abstinence for us. Most neighborhood children abstained from candy during Lent, and we were no exception. However, we really never missed out on any sweets offered to us. Before Ash Wednesday, each one of us obtained a shoe box to store the sweets that might fall into our hands during the six weeks of penance.

"What's all this?" demanded Mama one day as she cleaned the shelves in the children's clothes closet.

"It's my Lent candy," I explained, grabbing my treasure box off of the trash heap.

"Throw it out," Mama ordered mercilessly. "We'll have bugs and moths all over the place.

The clothes closet is no place for food, especially sweet, sticky stuff like this!"

We should have known better than to try to hide anything those days before Easter. Our house was always thoroughly scrubbed and cleaned to make ready for Resurrection Day. Nothing was safe from broom and the scrub brush, and Mama's eagle eye, especially the one in back of her head. (Mama always seemed to know when we got into mischief, even when her back was turned. She always told us that she had a third eye in the back of her head, as did all other mothers of small children. I guess we believed her, if she said so.)

"Throw this one out, too," said Mama as she tossed my little sister's Lent box on the heap. "You kids can't eat that stale, old stuff. Besides, you know that you can have as much fresh candy as you want anytime." This was really not a true statement since "as much as we wanted anytime" would have made us sick most of the time.

I remember carrying both boxes of goodies to the basement that day, carefully finding a new hiding place to store our sweet savings. It would only be a few more days before Easter. Then we would be able to enjoy the fruits of our sacrifices. There was no sweeter taste anywhere in the world than the anticipation of that hard, stale loot, stored away in our lenten shoe box.

"Allelulia, allelulia! Let the loud hosannas ring!" Those hosannas were loud and thrilling even at five o'clock on a very cold Easter morning. Our Easter always started with the first church service of Easter. The glorious music announcing "Christ is risen" was the climax of the long sobering Lenten season.

The mile-long trek home from church was full of happy anticipation. The Easter basket hunt began the minute we got home. I shall never forget the year that Toby, our big shaggy shepherd dog found our baskets first. He must have begun his hunt as soon as we left for church that morning. Even our disappointment couldn't cover up the amusing sight Toby made lying guilty and quiet in the middle of the mess he had made of all those lovely Easter nests, sick as a dog!

Breakfast on Easter morning was a meal to remember. Usually, some of our cousins, aunts and uncles came along to our house from church. The exciting Easter hunt went on while Mama was busy frying bacon and scrambling eggs. The table was full of the baked goods Mama had made on Holy Saturday.

As we all took our places at the table, Papa led the grace and asked God's blessing for our health and happiness, and prayed that we would all be together again for another Easter.

God Painting

He will raise his sacred hand
To paint pictures over sea and land.
His pictures will never grow old,
Hues of green, blue, silver and gold.
The moon with its soft silver light,
The stars a golden glow at night.
With the passing of the winter hours,
He will paint color on glorious flowers,
Then the birds in harmony will sing
When God paints in the spring.

Julia Swanson

God the Artist

God, when you thought of a pine tree,
   How did you think of a star?
God, when you patterned a birdsong,
   Flung on a silver string,
How did you know the ecstasy
   That crystal call would bring?
How did you think of a bubbling throat
   And a beautifully speckled wing?

God, when you fashioned a raindrop,
   How did you think of a stem
Bearing a lovely satin leaf
   To hold the tiny gem?
How did you know a million drops
   Would deck the morning's hem?

Why did you mate the moonlit night
   With the honeysuckle vines?
How did you know Madeira bloom
   Distilled ecstatic wines?
How did you weave the velvet dusk
   Where tangled perfumes are?
God, when you thought of a pine tree,
   How did you think of a star?

Angela Morgan

Photograph opposite
Mount Rainier National Park,
Washington
Freelance Photographers Guild

Who Loves
the Rain

Who loves the rain
    And loves his home,
And looks on life with quiet eyes,
    Him will I follow through the storm;
And at his hearth fire keep me warm;
    Nor hell nor heaven shall that soul surprise,
Who loves the rain,
    And loves his home,
And looks on life with quiet eyes.

Frances Shaw

Rain

The rain is raining all around,
It falls on field and tree,
It rains on the umbrellas here,
And on the ships at sea.

Robert Louis Stevenson

It's Spring

The reeds have ceased their rattling sound
And tracks appear in softened ground;
The whistling of the peepers bring
The entrance of an early spring.
Now pushing up the meadow's edge
Are crocuses beneath the hedge;
A million buds are coming out,
Forsythia blooming all about.
A sense of kinship swiftly brings
A love for all these growing things,
And in the doorway where I stand,
Enchanted by the greening land,
With all the riches of a king,
My heart cries out,
"It's spring, it's spring!"

Ralph M. J. Worth

Photograph opposite
Gunston Hall
Lorton, Virginia
Three Lions, Inc.

To a Skylark

Percy Bysshe Shelley

Hail to thee, blithe spirit!
Bird thou never wert,
That from heaven, or near it,
Pourest thy full heart
In profuse strains
Of unpremeditated art.

Higher still and higher
From the earth thou springest,
Like a cloud of fire;
The blue deep thou wingest,
And singing still dost soar,
And soaring ever singest.

In the golden lightning
Of the sunken sun,
O'er which clouds are brightening,
Thou dost float and run,
Like an unbodied joy
Whose race is just begun.

The pale purple even
Melts around thy flight;
Like a star of heaven,
In the broad daylight
Thou art unseen,
But yet I hear thy shrill delight,

Keen as are the arrows
Of that silver sphere,
Whose intense lamp narrows
In the white dawn clear,
Until we hardly see,
We feel that it is there.

All the earth and air
With thy voice is loud,
As, when night is bare,
From one lonely cloud
The moon rains out her beams,
And heaven is overflowed.

What thou art we know not;
What is most like thee?
From rainbow clouds there flow not
Drops so bright to see,
As from thy presence showers
A rain of melody.

Like a poet hidden
In the light of thought,
Singing hymns unbidden,
Till the world is wrought
To sympathy with hopes and fears
It heeded not;

Like a highborn maiden
In a palace tower,
Soothing her love-laden
Soul in secret hour
With music sweet as love,
Which overflows her bower;

Like a glowworm golden
In a dell of dew,
Scattering unbeholden
Its aerial hue
Among the flowers and grass,
Which screen it from the view;

What objects are the fountains
Of thy happy strain?
What fields or waves or mountains?
What shapes of sky or plain?
What love of thine own kind?
What ignorance of pain?

With thy clear keen joyance
Languor cannot be;
Shadow of annoyance
Never came near thee;
Thou lovest, but ne'er knew
Love's sad satiety.

Waking or asleep,
Thou of death must deem
Things more true and deep
Than we mortals dream,
Or how could thy notes flow
In such a crystal stream?

Like a rose embowered
In its own green leaves,
By winds deflowered,
Till the scent it gives
Makes faint with too much sweet
These heavy-winged thieves.

We look before and after,
And pine for what is not;
Our sincerest laughter
With some pain is fraught;
Our sweetest songs are those
That tell of saddest thought.

Sound of vernal showers,
On the twinkling grass,
Rain-awakened flowers,
All that ever was
Joyous and clear and fresh
Thy music doth surpass.

Yet if we could scorn
Hate and pride and fear;
If we were things born
Not to shed a tear,
I know not how thy joy
We ever should come near.

Teach us, sprite or bird,
What sweet thoughts are thine!
I have never heard
Praise of love or wine
That panted forth a flood
Of rapture so divine.

Better than all measures
Of delightful sound,
Better than all treasures
That in books are found,
Thy skill to poet were,
Thou scorner of the ground!

Chorus hymeneal
Or triumphal chant,
Matched with thine, would be all
But an empty vaunt,
A thing wherein we feel
There is some hidden want.

Teach me half the gladness
That thy brain must know,
Such harmonious madness
From my lips would flow,
The world should listen then,
As I am listening now.

Each Spring,
God Renews His Promise

Helen Steiner Rice

Long, long ago
   in a land far away,
There came the dawn
   of the first Easter Day.
And each year we see
   that promise reborn
That God gave the world
   on that first Easter Morn.
For in each waking flower
   and each singing bird,
The promise of Easter
   is witnessed and heard,
And spring is God's way
   of speaking to men
And renewing the promise
   of Easter again.
For death is a season
   that man must pass through
And, just like the flowers,
   God wakens him, too.
So why should we grieve
   when our loved ones die,
For we'll meet them again
   in a "cloudless sky";
For Easter is more
   than a beautiful story,
It's the promise of life
   and eternal glory.

Photograph opposite
Fred Sieb

The Strife is O'er

The strife is o'er, the battle done;
The victory of life is won;
The song of triumph has begun,
    Hallelujah!

The powers of death have done their worst,
But Christ their legions hath dispersed;
Let shout of holy joy outburst,
    Hallelujah!

The three sad days have quickly sped;
He rises glorious from the dead;
All glory to our risen Head!
    Hallelujah!

He brake the age-bound chains of hell;
The bars from heaven's high portals fell;
Let hymns of praise his triumph tell!
    Hallelujah!

Lord, by the stripes which wounded thee,
From death's dread sting thy servants free,
That we may live and sing to thee,
    Hallelujah!

Author Unknown

"The Strife Is O'er" is a well-known Easter hymn and was composed by Giovanni Pierluigi. Pierluigi studied music for many years, and served as choirmaster to a church in his native Palestrina, Italy. Eventually he was invited to sing in the Sistine Chapel Choir in Rome, which led to his appointment as choirmaster to the Papal Choir. In 1564, the Council of Trent commissioned Pierluigi to compose new music for the Mass, at which time he created the music for three Masses, and would write many more in the years to come. Giovanni Pierluigi has been called the "Prince of Music" because of the purity of his musical compositions. Greatly loved and honored throughout Italy, his music has also received international acclaim.

Jeweled Windows

The somber shadows of this sacred place
Are splashed with color, stained with gorgeous light:
The leaded windows shake their sun-filled lace
Upon the altar rail, and touch with bright
Quick fingers those who worship here.
These clean-cut jewels are as bright and clear
As amethysts and rubies—this pure green
Is like an emerald fire raining down,
Where Christ is pictured in the Easter scene.
There is a pearl-white cross, a gem-wrought crown,
And here the Shepherd with his gentle look;
And one slim panel holds the Holy Book.

A window to the west has caught the sun,
Where the Master kneels in dark Gethsemane,
The long road ended, and his great task done,
His patient eyes upraised in agony—
So close this window presses on my heart
I am one with him, I have become a part
Of every living thing—for there the Christ,
Kneeling in a light that does not dim,
Still has the same sure power that has sufficed
Through centuries to draw mankind to him.

Grace Noll Crowell

DONATED BY
Mr. Mrs. Peter Elsen Sr.

DONATED BY
Mr. Mrs. Peter Clavadini Jr.

Michelangelo

In March 1475, Michelangelo Buonarroti, an artist of great genius, was born. This artistic giant was to produce great masterpieces not only as a sculptor, but also as a painter and architect. Michelangelo would become the epitome of the Renaissance man. He was called the "Divine Michelangelo" for never before in the history of mankind had there appeared such a genius.

As a boy, Michelangelo was raised in genteel poverty by a family who had no regard for his talent or ambitions as an artist. Often, his father and uncles would beat him for bringing the shame of art to his family. As a boy of only thirteen, however, Michelangelo began his formal training as an artist in Florence, Italy. He exhibited a remarkable independence from his teachers and from contemporary influential artists, remaining true to his own spirit.

When Michelangelo was twenty-three years of age, he received a commission to sculpt a *Pieta*, which is now housed in St. Peter's Basilica in Rome. The *Pieta* took one year to complete. This masterpiece of his youth would become the treasure of St. Peter's and the world.

Ideals' Pages
from the Past

On the following six pages,
we are presenting a selection
from Easter Ideals 1947.

EASTER

ideals

He Passed This Way

By *Letitia Morse Nash*

He passed this way, and sleeping Earth
   Springs into life beneath His feet;
The seeds and bulbs that dormant lay
   Send forth a message, green and sweet.
The hard, bare trees that for long months
   Gave not a sign of growth or life
Burst into leaf and blossom fair,
   And all the Earth with joy is rife.
Tall Easter lilies, white and fair
   Proclaim the triumph of our King,
He passed this way, and all the Earth
   Shall joyously His praises sing.

He passed this way, and stumbling feet
   Walk straight and sure because He came.
And hands that faltered at their task
   Are blessed and strengthened in His name.
He makes the groping blind to see,
   The deaf to hear, the dumb to speak;
And brings a blessing of sweet peace
   To troubled ones that comfort seek.
He heals the broken hearts of men,
   And does their haunting fears allay.
And Earth may hope this Eastertime
   Because our Savior passed this way.

In all this cold and hollow world, no fount of deep, strong, deathless love save that within a mother's heart.

—Siege of Valencia

All I am, or can be, I owe to my angel mother.

—Abraham Lincoln

Who ran to help me when I fell,
And would some pretty story tell,
Or kiss the place to make it well? My mother.

—Jane Taylor

God could not be everywhere, and therefore he made mothers.

—Old Jewish Saying

An ounce of mother is worth a pound of clergy.

—Spanish Proverb

The instructions received at the mother's knee—are never entirely effaced from the soul.

—Lamennais

The babe at first feeds upon the mother's bosom, but it is always on her heart.

—Henry Ward Beecher

A man never sees all that his mother has been to him until it is too late.

—W. D. Howells

Some folks die too easy—they sort of fade away;
Make a little error, and give up in dismay;
Kind of man that's needed is the man of ready wit,
To laugh at pain and trouble and keep up his grit.

— *Louis E. Thayer.*

❀

Where you can't remove an obstacle, plow around it.

— *A. Lincoln*

❀

Try to obtain all of the facts before forming or expressing an opinion.

— *Martin Vanbee*

❀

Give to the world the best you have and the best will come back to you.

— *Anon.*

❀

Honor thy father and thy mother that thy days may be long upon the land which the Lord thy God giveth thee.

— *Exodus 20:12*

❀

The greatest hope of future society is individual character now.

— *W. E. Channing*

❀

A successful man is one who has tried, not cried; who has worked, not dodged; who has shouldered responsibility, not evaded it; who has gotten under the burden instead of standing off, looking on and giving advice.

— *Elbert Hubbard*

To Spring

By Revah Summersgill

O green and lovely season, dressed
In tender hues, you are the best,
The fairest of all lovely days!
Whether we wander woodland ways
Or sail the seas or walk along
A city's streets, your breath, your song,
Your deep sky with its high stars burning,
Your age-old miracles returning,
Your flowering and fragrant air
Spread God's own goodness everwhere!

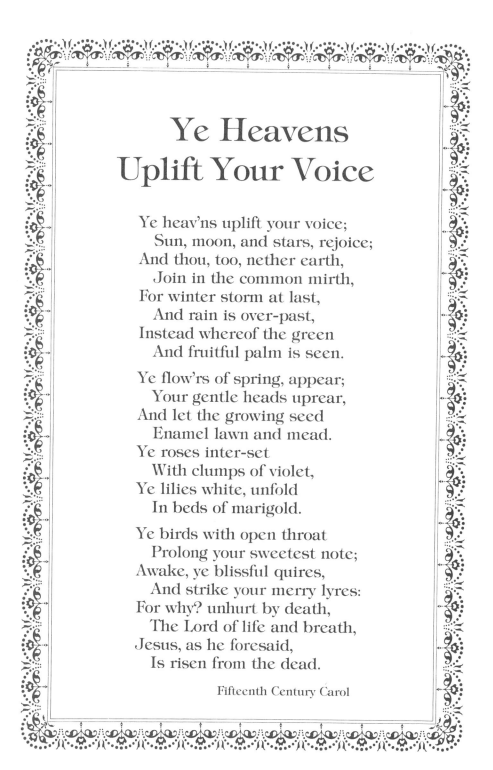

Ye Heavens
Uplift Your Voice

Ye heav'ns uplift your voice;
   Sun, moon, and stars, rejoice;
And thou, too, nether earth,
   Join in the common mirth,
For winter storm at last,
   And rain is over-past,
Instead whereof the green
   And fruitful palm is seen.

Ye flow'rs of spring, appear;
   Your gentle heads uprear,
And let the growing seed
   Enamel lawn and mead.
Ye roses inter-set
   With clumps of violet,
Ye lilies white, unfold
   In beds of marigold.

Ye birds with open throat
   Prolong your sweetest note;
Awake, ye blissful quires,
   And strike your merry lyres:
For why? unhurt by death,
   The Lord of life and breath,
Jesus, as he foresaid,
   Is risen from the dead.

Fifteenth Century Carol

Coming in Mother's Day Ideals—

The History of Mother's Day . . . a feature on carnations as a symbol of motherly virtues . . . an interesting look at Mothering Sunday, a 19th-century day in honor of Mother . . . Ideals Best-Loved Poet, Phyllis C. Michael . . . Pages from the Past, Mother's Day Ideals, 1948 . . . along with poetry and prose to honor Mother on her special day.

ACKNOWLEDGMENTS

EACH SPRING GOD RENEWS HIS PROMISE by Helen Steiner Rice. Used with permission of the author. WHO LOVES THE RAIN by Frances Shaw. First appeared in POETRY, copyright 1914 by The Modern Poetry Association. Reprinted by permission of the Editor of POETRY. RAIN by Robert Louis Stevenson. From A CHILD'S GARDEN OF VERSES by Robert Louis Stevenson. (Charles Scribner's Sons 1917). THE FLOWERS OF EASTER by Nancy Byrd Turner. Copyrighted. Used by permission of Melvin Lee Steadman, Jr. Our sincere thanks to the following authors whose addresses we were unable to locate: Carolyn Sherwin Bailey for MR. EASTER RABBIT; Julia Swanson for GOD PAINTING; Ralph M. J. Worth for IT'S SPRING.

Additional Photo Credits: Front cover, Fred Sieb. Inside front cover, Colleen Callahan Gonring. Inside back cover, Fred Sieb. Back cover, Fred Sieb.

ideals
PUBLISHING CORPORATION
11315 WATERTOWN PLANK RD.
MILWAUKEE, WISCONSIN 53226

Order the 2 New IDEALS For '79 Now . . .
Save Nearly 1/3 OFF

As our editor has told you, Ideals is adding two new issues to its 1979 line-up of beautiful reading. In March, the full color beauty of springtime couples with loving sentiments for Mom in our first Mother's Day Ideals. Later, in August, Autumn Ideals vividly portrays the rich earthtone colors of fall in this delightful expression of nature's most striking season.

But now's the time to reserve your special copies of these two exciting issues . . . and if you act now, you'll **SAVE 32% OFF** the regular newsstand price.

Ideals now carries a cover price of $2.95 a copy and $16.00 for a one-year (8 issue) subscription—$28.00 for a two-year (16 issue) subscription.

To increase your current subscription to the full eight issues, you may now order the new Mother's Day and Autumn issues for just $4.00, a savings of over 32% from the newsstand price. Send your order now and the two new issues will be sent to you as released, thus increasing your subscription to the new basis of eight issues.

Remove this envelope form, add your name and address and enclose your check for $4.00 or charge as you wish. Upon receipt we will immediately upgrade your current subscription to include the two new issues scheduled in 1979.

Look for more good news from Ideals in the coming months—new and improved Ideals with things to do and places to enjoy, along with all the beautiful photos, paintings, poetry and prose you expect in every issue of Ideals.

---

ideals
PUBLISHING CORPORATION
11315 WATERTOWN PLANK RD.
MILWAUKEE, WISCONSIN 53226

☐ Enclosed check or money order
Bill to: ☐ Visa ☐ Master Charge
Credit Card No. _____
Exp. Date _____
If Master Charge enter 4 digit Interbank
No. _____
Signature _____

I Don't Want To Miss An Issue . . .
Here Is My Order For The
2 Additional Issues in 1979

YES Please enter my order for the two new Ideals editions to be published in 1979—"Mother's Day Ideals" and "Autumn Ideals" which I understand will be sent when published—in March and August, respectively.

Name _____
Address _____
City _____ State _____ Zip _____

FOLD SIDE FLAPS FIRST

When properly sealed with the above gummed flap this envelope and its contents will travel safely through the mail.

FOLD HERE FIRST

BE94

FOLD SIDE FLAPS FIRST — THEN FOLD HERE

ideals PUBLISHING CORPORATION
11315 WATERTOWN PLANK RD.
MILWAUKEE, WISCONSIN 53226

( )
ZIP CODE

from

THANK YOU!

FOLD HERE FIRST